American Realism

Poems By

Pamela Martin

American Realism
Copyright 2008 by Pamela Gowan

All rights reserved under International and Pan-American copyright conventions. No part of this book may be reproduced, stored in a retrieval system or transmitted in any form, electronic, mechanical, or by any other means, without written permission of the author.

International Standard Book Number: 978-0-615-26121-8

Illustrated by Kathleen Hardy.

Table of Contents

Part I

Ready or Not	9
Plagiarism	9
Finders Keepers	9
Elucubrate!	10
Forlorn	10
O.C.D.	10
Enchantment	11
Reservations	12
Conversation Piece	12
Hierarchy	12
Heliocentrism	13
Digamy	14
Trading Places	14
Ineffable	14
Regina	15
Letter-perfect	16
Pillow Talk	16
Natatorium	16
Lyre, Lyre	17
Eavesdrop	18
The Odyssey Continues	18
A Vicious Cycle	18
Epigone	19
Personal Best	20
Wishful Thinking	20
Resolution	20
Agoraphobia	21
Greetings!	21
Pre-Texting	21
Pettiness	22
Down a Slippery Slope	22
Faux pas	22
Coffee Mate	23
Genre	23
The Hippodrome	23

Part II

Beton brut	27
Brook No Evil	27
What a Dickens!	27
Duped	28
Femme fatale	28
Francophobia	28
Don Juan	29
Taurus	30
Alma Mater	30
Stalk Her	30
Culture	31
Parabolic Inequalities	32
While Mighty Oaks Do Fall	32
Are We There Yet?	32
American Realism	33
Hang Together	34
WWJD?	34
Opening Statements	34
Desperately Seeking???	35
The Dark Ages	36
Chanteuse	36
Shell Shock	36
An Inconvenient Truth	37
Fatalism	38
Statute of Limitations	38
An Undercover Job	38
The Preoccupation	39
Let There Be Light!	39
Doggerel	39
Rent-A-Poem	40
Wardrobe Consultant	40
Misercordia	40
Repressed Memory	41
Interdigitation	41
Madame Curious	41

Part III

Make Haste 45
Presentism 45
The Omen 45
Good vs. Evil 46
Lucky Guy 46
A Busy Intersection 46
Dust Jackets 47
Wherefore? 48
General Consensus 48
Bee My Friend 48
The Cooking Jean 49
William F. Buckley Jr. (1925-2008) 50
Bartholomew, the cat. 50
Cuckold 50
Baccalaureate 51
Confucius: 52
Delete 52
Absinthe 52
The Little Mermaid 53
Solitary Confinement 54
Historical Irony 54
The Labor of Sisyphus 54
T.M.I. 55
Cephalization 56
Apotheosis 56
Tonal Harmony 56
Conditional Clauses 57
A Bathing Suit 57
In Possession of a Controlled Substance 57
Mind over Matter 58
No Alibi 58
Plato's Academy 58
M.B.A. 59
Ethereal Message. 59
Who's Counting 59
Ecumenism 60
Historicist. 60
En passant 60

Part I

Ready or Not

Grand theft auto
And petty larceny
Make a rich man humble
And a poor man free.
But, like the wily pickpocket,
The thief in the night
Will take your soul
Without a fight.

Plagiarism

If I did not know better,
I would be appalled
To think that it was my work
They easily recalled
By the name of someone
Who never knew the pain
Of giving birth to something
He could not explain.

Finders Keepers

Philosophy and history
Have always been fast friends.
Philosophy tells us
"The means justify the ends."
History tells us
"Time is undefined."
And together they tell us
"Seek and ye shall find."

Elucubrate!

We believe many things
That simply are not true.
I believe that you believe them.
I believe them, too.
There is nothing wrong with
Speaking what is right
But there is something wrong with
Extinguishing the light.

Forlorn

Time and time again
Love has passed me by.
I can't help but wonder
If I should even try
To give up the ghosts
Of my former ambition
Or beat my desires
Into total submission.

O.C.D.*

If I had a cell phone,
I'd call every day.
I'd call in the morning
Much to your dismay.
If I had a whistle,
I'd whistle all the time.
I'd whistle in the evening
Until supper time.

*Obsessive-Compulsive Disorder.

Enchantment

Tabby is a mendicant.
She begs all the time
At the dinner table.
It really is a crime.
But to those of us who know her
We know she means no harm.
And, when you think about it,
It adds to her sweet charm.

Reservations

I wound you
And you wound me.
We will heal
Eventually.
But in this land
Of bigotry,
We still have
Our Wounded Knee.

Conversation Piece

The truth is there is no truth
But we love it just the same.
We love it as if it were
One of our old flames.
To love something that doesn't exist
Is a bit surreal.
But we do it all the time.
Love is so unreal.

Hierarchy

All men are created equal
Except for you and me.
We're a cut above the rest.
It's sheer hypocrisy.
Inequality is a fact.
No one can deny it.
Only in democracy
Would we even try it.

Heliocentrism

Every waking minute
Of every waking hour
I look to the sun
To give me the power
To live my life
As I see fit
And to make
The most of it.

Digamy

I once told a lie
That became the truth.
The lie I once told
I told in Bayreuth.
I once told a truth
That became a lie.
I'll always love you.
Why did you have to die?

Trading Places

If I had a dollar
For every time you said,
"What is it you're thinking
In that pretty head?"
I would be Paris Hilton
As flush as flush can be.
But could Paris Hilton
Ever be me?

Ineffable

You know I know you love me.
You were always there.
You know the more I love you
The more you know I care.
But the less I say the better.
Words cannot convey
The way I feel about you
Is the way I'll feel always.

Regina*

Oh, to be a Jezebel,
A painted, tainted ne'er-do-well
Who Elijah did foretell
Was eaten by the dogs.
But cast aspersions to the wind.
Who of us has not sinned
And in our hearts does not rescind
The golden Decalogue?

*Latin, "Queen."

Letter-perfect

The time for change is never done
Though subtle change may be
In the person you've become,
Your personality.
When change is good, it is said
It is for the better.
When change is bad, it is said
It is by the letter.

Pillow Talk

I took another sleep aid
So I could go to sleep.
It knocked me out in seconds
And put me under deep.
I laughed when someone told me
Even an O.T.C.
Can be as dangerously addictive
As using Ecstasy.

Natatorium

Softly flow the Shiloh waters.
Gently winds the River Styx.
Slowly creeps the shore's advancing.
Loudly churns the confluence mix.
Send to me your lame and dying.
Send to me your blind.
Send them to Bethesda's pool,
A miracle to find.

Lyre, Lyre

Odysseus heard the siren song.
They tied him to the mast.
They sang it to him all night long.
He wished that it would last.
The Argonauts were wiser men.
They heard the sirens not
But listened to sweet Orpheus,
The man who time forgot.

Eavesdrop

If you listen carefully,
You will learn a lot
About things you don't understand
Like what means "Aeroflot".
Some things you don't need to know.
Just file them away.
You can never know too much
On a rainy day.

The Odyssey Continues

You can bowdlerize and sanitize
And censor all you want.
You can expurgate and bifurcate.
You can even taunt.
But one thing is for certain.
You can never break
The spirit of adventure
Which I cannot forsake.

A Vicious Cycle

I'm passively aggressive
When it comes to you
And actively aggressive
To a chosen few.
But when I'm quietly submissive,
I am much aggrieved
By the very people
I have just reprieved.

Epigone

I am a living scion
Of a patrician family.
I do as I am told
To promote true harmony.
If I could make the mummies dance
Or earn a single penny
I would please some
And surprise many.

Personal Best

In all honesty,
Writing is a drag
Especially to the author
Who does not like to brag.
Anyone can do it
Better than you.
And then you get the feeling
You can, too.

Wishful Thinking

I wished for snow
And down it fell.
And it was
As cold as hell.
But when I wish
For diamond rings,
I usually
Get other things.

Resolution

Does the word intransigent
Mean anything to you?
Do unrelenting and inflexible
Ring a bell or two?
Resolute is the term
I know you prefer.
I intend to use it here
Exactly as it were.

Agoraphobia

Cloistered and secluded,
I live my life alone.
Rarely do I ever
Leave my prison home.
But I have adventures
Vicarious though they be.
The National Geographic
Has come to rescue me.

Greetings!

I don't like to think a lot.
If I think at all,
It's usually something I regret
I do not recall.
What little I remember
I try to forget.
If I am successful,
We have never met.

Pre-Texting

DNA and T&A
Are all you need to CYA
If you work for the CIA
Or undercover DEA.

Pettiness

Sammy is a "pet" whore.
She wants it all the time.
"Won't you, please, just pet me?"
Is her favorite chime.
She wants us both to take her
To the petting zoo
Because that's where, she tells us,
All her dreams come true.

Down A Slippery Slope

It hurts to say I'm sorry.
But I must take the blame
For what I said about you.
You would do the same.
We are at an impasse
In our relationship.
Whatever we do now,
We can't afford to slip.

Faux pas*

I am disappointed
At the very least.
You did not invite me
To your fancy feast.
An apology's in order
But do not pretend
That I could ever be
Your dinner guest again.

*French, lit. false step, social blunder.

Coffee Mate

I heard it was over.
You went your separate ways.
I can't help but wonder
If this is just a phase.
Do you breakup to makeup?
If this is true,
When will you wakeup
And smell the morning brew?

Genre

Poetry is a language
I'd don't speak very well.
The words don't come easy.
The rhyming is hell.
So, why do I do it?
It is a game
I can play every morning
And still use my brain.

The Hippodrome

We went to the races.
The stands were filled
With drunken horse lovers
Whose brains were distilled.
When it was over
(and that was too soon),
They kept right on drinking
All afternoon.

Part II

Beton brut*

In Moscow and St. Petersburg
Whose streets are very wide.
It takes a long, long time
To get to the other side.
When at last you get there,
You will be depressed
Because the modern architecture of Russia
Will leave you unimpressed.

*French, "raw concrete," unfinished concrete left exposed visually.

Brook No Evil

Time has been good to you.
Fate has been kind.
You have been blessed
With a beautiful mind.
Use it for something
You can be sure
Will always be something
Sacred and pure.

What a Dickens!

My favorite novelist
Is Charles Dickens.
Picaresque themes
Are slim-pickens.
With every twist
The plot thickens.
When I read him,
My heart quickens.

Duped

You took me down the garden path.
Boy, was I naïve.
If I did not know better,
I think I was deceived.
I can't believe I trusted
You implicitly
And, for what its worth,
Inexplicably.

Femme fatale

Do you find me intriguing?
Is it my mystique?
Or my silken stockings
Bought at a boutique?
Do my undergarments
Really turn you on?
Or these two voluptuous ladies
Filled with silicon?

Francophobia

I've never been to Paris
And I never want to go.
I don't like the weather
Especially when it snows.
The food there can be tasty
If you like the sauce.
If not I'm afraid
It is a total loss.

Don Juan

Give the boot to Italy
And the Sicilian mob.
They would give up willingly
If they had a job.
Work is noble. Work is good.
Pull out the cork.
And then we'll move on
To the streets of New York.

Taurus

I was a bull in a china shop
Selling Tupperware.
If you don't believe me
You should have been there.
The china was so fragile
Sitting on the shelf.
The Tupperware was wantonly
Tossed from elf to elf.

Alma Mater

We can finish college
Only if we die.
We can never give up
That old "college try."
Receiving a diploma
Is the first plateau
That leads us to where
We want to go.

Stalk Her

It sure took a long to miss me.
It sure took a long time to care.
It sure took a long time to notice
That I would not always be there.
If you are somewhat belated
In showing your feelings for me,
I am still super elated.
You are my fantasy.

Culture

The cult of domesticity
Is no cult at all.
It's the battle of the sexes,
Your basic barroom brawl.
It is a religion
Women worship every day
As they cook and clean
Without any pay.

Parabolic Inequalities

Amazon women invented
The single mastectomy,
A sacrifice they made
For certain victory.
Amazon men invented
A curved trajectory
That would not require
A simple vasectomy.

While Mighty Oaks Do Fall

There are so many things that can kill us.
It's a wonder we are alive.
In all of our human existence,
Only the strong have survived.
But no one was stronger than Samson.
No one was stronger than Hercules.
No one was stronger than Goliath
(Although David brought him down to his knees).

Are We There Yet?

The beauty of the cosmos
Is more logical
Than all the theorems and apothegms
You find farcical.
If what we are lacking
Is indeed irrational,
Aren't we all just travelers
Getting emotional?

"American Realism"

Abraham was honest,
Honest to a fault.
But never did he ever
"Enter" Mrs. Galt.
No matter what he did,
He couldn't tell a lie.
That is how we know
He ate that cherry pie.

"Hang Together"

If you do not stand up
And fight for what is right
You may even lose
Your innate right to fight.
The pallor of your valor
Will tell you what to do
And will give to you the courage
To speak that which is true.

WWJD?*

You would if you loved me.
You would if you cared.
Why do I feel
Mentally impaired?
Perplexed and confounded,
I'm so confused.
You made me an offer
I couldn't refuse.

*What Would Jesus Do?

Opening Statements

Prosecution:
"There is every indication
That your insubordination
Is a great abomination
And a criminal offense."

Defense:
"But if you will tread lightly
And pray for us nightly
And adjudicate rightly,
We have a valid defense."

Desperately Seeking???

I was lucky to have met you
In the fast car lane.
And, if luck would have it,
I'd meet you there again.
You slowed down to drag race
And shouted out your name
Which, I must confess,
I did not retain.

The Dark Ages

Before the lamp post
It was dark
Especially walking
In the park.
We thrashed about
Until three
Or until
We could see.

Chanteuse

Karen* was a superstar
More than words can tell.
She sang of the love and heartache
We know all too well.
She was starved for affection
And carbohydrates, too.
And yet anorexia
Is still a cultural taboo.

*Karen Carpenter (1950-1983); female vocalist and drummer.

Shell Shock

We have fought the good fight.
And we have lost.
We can't say for certain
At what cost.
The number of weary.
The number of dead.
The number of soldiers
Sick in the head.

An Inconvenient Truth

The furnaces of hell
Are working overtime
And fire up whenever
You commit a crime.
If some like it hot,
This is an extreme.
In this day and age,
Even the devil's going green.

Fatalism

Love is lost
And love is found
In every village
And every town.
Who of us
Can escape
The certainty
Of such a fate?

Statute of Limitations

I took an oath
To tell the truth
About the errors
Of my youth.
But when I think
About the past
I know the die
Was never cast.

An Undercover Job

Any *agent provocateur*
Would hop at the chance
To expose a fellow agent
In an illicit romance.
They know the spy who loved her
Also sold her crystal meth.
Retribution would come swiftly,
As swiftly as her death.

The Preoccupation

Heart of hearts
Hear me out.
Listen closely.
I won't shout.
All that you.
Need to know
Is that I
Will never go.

Let There Be Light!

Incandescent, luminescent,
Fluorescent, UV
Illuminate the world
So we can see.
But Thomas Edison
Could not have known
What we'd do
When we're not alone.

Doggerel

I've got time on my hands
And bells on my toes.
Believe it or not
Anything goes.
Someone once said,
"Enough is enough."
Who am I
To call his bluff?

Rent-a-Poem

If your halo gives you
Ring-around-the-collar,
It's because you worship
The-almighty-dollar.
But there's no need to
Scream and holler.
I'm paid upfront,
Not by the hour.

Wardrobe Consultant

Let me assist you.
Let me assess
How you're looking
In that dress.
Let me see,
What's your size?
Let me show off
My merchandise.

Misercordia*

In this day of
Drunken rages
We still need
Our learned sages
Not to tell us
How to live
But to show
How to forgive.

*Latin, "mercy."

Repressed Memory

If my youth was
Misbegotten,
At least now it is
Forgotten.
I will not go
To a place
Where there is no
Saving grace.

Interdigitation

Nihilism and pessimism
Go hand in hand.
Like liver and sausage
(which I cannot stand).
Nihilism is a kind of
Linear regression
And pessimism is a kind of
Tropical depression.

Madame Curious

A light went on
Inside her head
Made of
Radioactive lead.
When she got
Her first brain tumor
They said that it was
Just a rumor.
She aspires to the
Nobel Prize
Which she often does not
Realize.
Although she can't be
Madame Curie,
She can still be
Full of fury.

Part III

Make Haste

The clock on the wall keeps on ticking.
It tells me that I better quicken
My leisurely pace
And do it with grace
Or run around like a spring chicken.

Presentism

To live for the present
Is to live for today
Never letting the past
Get in your way.
But to live for the future
Is risky at best.
Heart disease can lead
To cardiac arrest.

The Omen

I had a presentiment,
A premonition of you,
An eerie foreboding
Out of the blue.
I closed my eyes
And counted to ten.
I opened my eyes,
And you were with them.

Good vs. Evil

Benevolence and malevolence
Could never coexist
In peaceful harmony
Or in peaceful bliss.
I can wish you well or ill.
You can do the same.
But you can't do them both at once.
It is a crying shame.

Lucky Guy

A more suitable match
Could not be found.
She was a princess
Wearing a crown.
You were a guy
Down on your luck
Who needed someone
To pick him up.

A Busy Intersection

I look to the left.
Then I look to the right.
I look up and down.
It is alright
To step from the curb,
And cross the street
And greet all the people
I chance to meet.

Dust Jackets

The things that we hold on to
Are the things we can't let go.
We hold on to them anyway
Because we need to know
That we are part of something
That is larger than ourselves
And will not be forgotten
Like tomes upon the shelves.

Wherefore?

It's Thursday morning.
I'm up before dawn.
Suddenly I
Begin to yawn.
It remains to me
A mystery
Why I studied
History.

General Consensus

"I'll show you my etchings."
"I'll show you the door.
Why do you think
I am a whore
And can be seduced
Into your bed?"
"Because that's what
The General said."

Bee My Friend

If I could
Do it again,
I would pick you
To be my friend
Not for love
Or for money
But because
You're sweet as honey.

The Cooking Jean

When it comes to cooking,
I do not.
I like my food served
Cold or hot.
Teach a man to fish
And he'll eat for life
But most of the time
He prefers a wife.

William F. Buckley Jr. (1925-2008)

There is nothing really special
About following the rules.
Anyone can do it.
Even us fools.
But iconoclasm counts
In our society
More than the conservative tradition
Of acting responsibly.

Bartholomew,* the cat

The chief difference between
Dogs and cats
Is that dogs are dogs
And cats are cats,
Beyond that there's
Not much to say
Except that cats are
Easier to flay.

*Bartholomew was a martyred saint (one of the twelve apostles), who was flayed to death as rendered in a tableau on the Sistine Chapel by Michelangelo.

Cuckold

I took pity on you
And gave you a chance.
You repaid me with
This contrivance.
Far be it for me
To be so ungrateful
But how could you
Be so unfaithful?

Baccalaureate

The liberal artist works the hardest
Just to get ahead.
I should know for I must go
And earn my daily bread.
Very often we will soften
As we mop the floor.
But deep inside we have our pride.
We are the working poor.

Confucius:

"Life won't wait.
So why should you?
There is still
So much to do.
Do it now,
And don't be late.
He is lost
Who hesitates."

"Delete"

I have lost the self-control
I have never had.
I acted so impulsively.
The things I did were bad.
But I did them anyway.
I have no regrets.
I did the very best I could.
The rest I will forget.

Absinthe

I have been oblivious
To your many faults.
For so long now I have had
To use smelling salts
To wake in the morning
And get out of bed
And grapple with the issues
That burn inside my head.

The Little Mermaid

If I were a mermaid,
I would have no feet.
My body would have scales
That would never leak.
But not all mermaids
Look like me.
They say that I look
Heavenly.

Solitary Confinement

We are autodidacts
When it comes to love.
The School for Scandal teaches
None of the above.
Only time will tell
If we get it right
Or banish us forever
From the chamber of the night.

Historical Irony

When you write about yourself
It's autobiography.
When you write nursery rhymes
It's a form of poetry.
When you write about the truth
It is irony.
But no matter what you write about
It is history.

The Labor of Sisyphus

"I wrote a book."
"I wrote ten."
The sword is mightier
Than the pen.
No matter how much
You may write,
You may never
Get it right.

T.M.I.*

We took command.
We took control.
It looked like
We were on a roll
Until they bombed
Our left flank
And rammed us
With an armored tank.

*Too Much Information.

Cephalization

If it weren't for the corpus callosum,
We wouldn't know right from left,
One hand couldn't wash the other,
We wouldn't be so deft.
The left brain is for language.
The right is for the arts.
No matter how you slice it
The brain has made us smart.

Apotheosis

I am not infallible.
I'm perfect in every way.
If you don't believe me,
Just ask my cousin Ray.
I never make mistakes.
I'm faultless to a fault.
I'm a paragon of virtue,
And I do somersaults.

Tonal Harmony

If you believe in love,
Don't dream about it.
Do what you must
And shout about it.
If you believe in music,
Don't talk about it.
Raise up your voice
And sing about it.
If you believe in me
As I do you,
There's nothing that
We can't do.

Conditional Clauses

If I told you how I feel,
You wouldn't understand.
No matter what you say or do
You are just a man.
If problems have solutions
That we can't ignore,
Then solutions have their problems
And a whole lot more.

A Bathing Suit

It took a while to save him.
They say he nearly drowned.
His lungs were filled with water.
In the bathroom he was found.
The manufacturer has issued a warning:
When you sleep at night,
Empty the bathtub completely
And never turn off the light.

In Possession of a Controlled Substance

There's nothing more for me to say
Than I loved you so.
I have loved you everyday
Since you let me go.
And I'll love you more and more
Until you finally see
That I belong to you,
And you belong to me.

Mind over Matter

At times the future
Seems bleak
Like when my boat
Springs a leak.
But, when it comes
To me and you,
We both know
Dreams come true.

No Alibi

His whereabouts are largely unknown.
Somebody called on the phone.
They didn't get through.
What could he do?
He spent the whole evening alone.

Plato's Academy

Vocabulary is the centerpiece
Of the literary arts.
Words are all you need
To sound so very smart.
But if perchance you fail
To develop verbally,
You should promptly sign up
For a language academy.

M.B.A.

Maximize your profits.
Minimize your debts.
When playing the stock market,
Always hedge your bets.
The Federal Reserve Board
Is your closest friend.
It dictates periodically
The rate at which you lend.

Ethereal Message

Eight lines do not do justice
To the subjects I review.
But justice is not my goal.
That is my point of view.
I like to travel lightly
Though you may like it not.
My themes come from the ether
Time has forgot.

Who's Counting?

I wrote 1,200 poems
Since 2004.
I do NOT
Want to write any more.
Emily wrote 1,700
In her lifetime.
They were also short
And were made for primetime.

Ecumenism

I'm not stereotyping.
Who would be typecast?
We know racial profiling
Is a thing of the past.
Rugged individualism is the
Bulwark of our faith
Without which our religion
Would be interfaith.

Historicist

I remember when stealing a horse
Was a capital offence.
When there was not a penny for tribute
But millions for defense.
When we lifted the tariff
On the English muffin.
When I knew the price of everything
But the value of nothing.

En passant*

Check the citations.
Consider the source.
Let the juggernauts
Run their course.
History is history.
The past is the past.
And our world
Is fading fast.

*French, "in passing."

www.ingramcontent.com/pod-product-compliance
Lightning Source LLC
LaVergne TN
LVHW011430080426
835512LV00005B/367